The Message of
St Thérèse of Lisieux

by
Rt Rev Mgr Vernon Johnson

*All booklets are published thanks to the
generous support of the members of the
Catholic Truth Society*

CATHOLIC TRUTH SOCIETY
PUBLISHERS TO THE HOLY SEE

CONTENTS

*The quotations in this pamphlet are taken from the Saint's
Autobiography, unless otherwise stated.*

THE MESSAGE OF ST THÉRÈSE OF LISIEUX

Has St Thérèse a particular message to the world? If so, what is it? To many Catholics this question has never arisen. To them St Thérèse is a Saint canonised by the Catholic Church and, as such, is proposed in some sense as a model for the faithful; but as to what that model exactly is they are by no means clear. Some again hold her in great devotion as the Saint from whom they have received great personal help and many favours which they describe as 'roses'. To others again this very devotion is distasteful; they dislike this talk of roses, it savours of the sentimental and picturesque, and they dislike sentiment, especially where religion is concerned: they prefer their own saints: St Thérèse is not for them, and they leave it at that.

A still greater number of people find a stumbling block in the word 'little'. They think it means something weak and feeble, whereas on the lips of St Thérèse the word 'little' expresses that complete dependence upon God which is the foundation of all spiritual greatness. The whole secret of the Little Way lies in the words of our Blessed Lord, 'Without me you can do nothing'.

These, one and all, miss the whole reason why God has raised up this particular Saint in our own particular time. What then is the message of St Thérèse? It is true that she said she would scatter roses on the earth, but she did not say that that was her Mission. What then is her Mission? Her Mission is to teach to the faithful her 'Little Way of Spiritual Childhood'.

THE LITTLE WAY OF SPIRITUAL CHILDHOOD

The Witness of the Saint

Towards the end of her last illness she said to her sister, Mother Agnes of Jesus: 'I feel that my Mission is soon to begin, my Mission to teach souls my little way'. Her sister asked her: 'What is the little way that you would teach to souls?' 'It is The Way of Spiritual Childhood, the way of trust and absolute self-surrender'. Was this sense of a Mission to teach her Little Way to souls a mere delusion, just an expression of pride? Or was it the prophecy of a divine Mission? Pope Benedict XV gives the answer: 'Since Sister Thérèse had been humble all her life, it could only have been by a divine inspiration that she spoke in her last moments in an apparently contrary sense'.

The Witness of Almighty God

When St Thérèse spoke these words concerning her Mission to teach her Little Way to souls she was hidden in her convent, utterly unknown to the world outside, not appreciated even by some of the sisters among whom she lived. No sooner had she died than her tomb became the scene of countless miracles. After the publication of her autobiography further miracles took place in every corner of the world in answer to the prayers of the faithful. Europe, America, Africa, India, and China, all gave their testimony to these miraculous happenings. In the words of Pius XI, St Thérèse became 'a prodigy of miracles'. God, by these miracles, is calling the attention of the faithful to the sanctity of St Thérèse, and to her particular type of sanctity, holding it up for the imitation of the faithful. So these endless miracles are simply Almighty God pointing the faithful to the Saint and saying: 'Look well, for this person comes from Me to teach you "the little way to spiritual childhood, the way of trust and absolute self-surrender".'

The Witness of the Church

So overwhelming was this avalanche of miracles and this world-wide devotion to the Saint that it resulted in an event till then most rare in the history of the Church. The period of fifty years which must elapse between the death and canonisation of a Saint was dispensed by the Holy See, and within twenty-eight years St Thérèse was a canonised Saint of the Catholic Church. In the process of canonisation two Sovereign Pontiffs have laboured to draw the attention of the faithful to the special message and Mission of the Saint. Benedict XV says: 'There is a call to the faithful of every nation, no matter what may be their age, sex, or state of life, to enter whole-heartedly into

the Little Way which led Sister Thérèse to the summit of
heroic virtue'. 'In spiritual childhood is the secret of
sanctity for *all* the faithful of the Catholic world'. 'It is
Our special desire that the secret of the sanctity of Sister
Thérèse of the Child Jesus may be revealed to all Our
children'. Pius XI is no less definite: 'We earnestly desire
that *all the faithful* should study her in order to copy her,
becoming children themselves; since otherwise they
cannot, according to the word of the Master, arrive at the
kingdom of heaven'. 'Let us listen to what little Thérèse
will tell us, she who has become a word of God'. These
words of Benedict XV and Pius XI clearly present St
Thérèse to the Universal Church as the authorised teacher
of her Little Way of Spiritual Childhood.

The Scriptural Foundation

It is embedded in the Sacred Scriptures. 'As your word
unfolds, it gives light, and the *little ones* understand' (*Ps*
119:130). 'The decree of the Lord is trustworthy, wisdom
for the *little ones*' (*Ps* 19:7). 'The Lord is the keeper of
little ones' (*Ps* 114:6). 'Whosoever is a *little one*, let him
come to me' (*Pr* 9:4). Listen to the prophet, 'The wolf
lives with the lamb, the panther lies down with the kid,
calf and lion cub feed together, with a *little one* to lead
them' (*Is* 11:6). A perfect parable of the spirit of
childhood taking the conflicting passions of human nature
and binding them into one harmonious whole. 'Like a son

comforted by his mother will I comfort you' (Is 66:13). So far the Old Testament. The New Testament is even more insistent, and the speaker is Our Lord Himself, 'I bless you, Father, Lord of heaven and of earth, for hiding these things from the learned and the clever and revealing them to the *little ones*' (*Mt* 11:25). 'Let the *little children* alone, and do not stop them coming to me; for it is to such as these that the kingdom of heaven belongs' (*Mt* 19:14). And supremely – 'Unless you change and become like *little children*, you will never enter the kingdom of heaven' (*Mt* 18:3). In view of these words Benedict XV says that Our Lord declared the way of spiritual childhood to be 'absolutely essential'.

THE NATURE OF THE LITTLE WAY

It was from these texts that St Thérèse drew the inspiration of her Little Way. She would be her heavenly Father's little child, and would act towards Him in her spiritual life exactly as a little child acts towards its parent in the natural life.

Let us now examine the foundations of this Little Way of Spiritual Childhood.

Love

In ordinary human life, what is the supreme relationship between a little child and its mother? It is love. It is the mother's love that has brought the little child into being, and by its mother's love it is supported every moment. Above all, the thing which the mother wants supremely from her little child is its love. If she possesses all else but does not possess that, her heart is left aching. Now, from the point of view of the little one, what does the little child want? It wants love. Without its mother's love it is not merely restless, it is completely lost. Again, in its helplessness the only gift that the little child can give to its mother is its love. Our Lord did not say 'Unless you be converted and become children'; He said 'little children'. In its littleness it can give only one thing, but that one thing is everything, namely, love. Between a mother and her child all is love, and if this should not exist, then all society cries out in horror that things are wrong.

Now in the supernatural life this is precisely theologically true. God is our heavenly Father. He has created us because He loves us. By His love we are supported every moment. The one thing which this heavenly Father wants from us, His children, is our love. Without it, His heart is left aching. We, on our side, we, His little children, we want supremely the love of our heavenly Father. Without it we are restless and dissatisfied. Why is the world so unhappy? Because it is trying to satisfy itself with something less than the love of God. We are made for that love of God, and we are restless till we rest within it. And, in return for this love, what can we give that will satisfy the heart of our heavenly Father? Only love. In our helplessness we are only able to give our love, and that is the one thing God wants. All our actions are only valuable in His eyes insofar as they are the expression of our love for Him. That is the foundation of the Little Way of Spiritual Childhood, it is all love. It begins in love, exists by love, and ends in love.

In the eyes of St Thérèse this was everything: 'My Little Way is all love'. Sometimes it is the love of her heavenly Father which absorbs her. Her continual cry was 'God thirsts for our love'. At the other times it is the love of her own heart; her love goes out in response to her

Father's love. 'Let us love', she writes, 'for love alone our hearts are made'. Sometimes it is the two together which captivate her soul. 'Oh, my God, I know it. Love is repaid by love alone. Therefore I have sought, I have found how to ease my heart by giving You love for love'.

In the natural sphere, where does a little child get its power to love? It is not a purely subjective emotion. The child depends for it entirely upon its mother. The capacity to love which exists in its little heart it owes to its mother's love; and this capacity is only quickened into action by the objective fact of its mother's love outside it. As it looks at its mother it cares nothing if she be rich, intelligent or beautiful. All it looks for is her love and, seeing its mother's love, its own little love is quickened into life. It is the same in the supernatural life. Our power to love God does not spring from a subjective emotion. It all depends on the objective fact of God's love for us, that love which has existed from all eternity, long before we were born. We depend upon Him for our existence, but, far more important still, we owe entirely to Him the capacity which we possess to love Him in the only way which can satisfy His heart. 'We are to love, then, because he loved us first' (*1 Jn* 4:19). That is the order. The little – that is to say, childlike – soul, who treads the Little Way, looking at its heavenly Father, puts aside all His other attributes, His omniscience, His omnipotence, and sees just one overwhelming thing, His love.

It was this that captivated the soul of St Thérèse. As she looked, with the eyes of a child, on the mysteries of the Faith – Bethlehem, Calvary, the Resurrection – they all spelt this one word, love. It was the heavenly Father's love coming down to earth to fill the soul of His little child with love and so lift it up to Him. To her the heavenly Father's love shone out in the Sacred Scriptures supremely in the words of our Blessed Lord: 'If anyone loves me he will keep my word, and my Father will love him, and we shall come to him, and make our home with him' (*Jn* 14:23). Here was the supreme gift of the heavenly Father's love, nothing less than the Holy Trinity dwelling in her soul; for where the Father and the Son come, there comes also the Holy Spirit. Her soul was the tabernacle of the Trinity. 'Oh, Trinity', she cried, 'You are the prisoner of my love'. The very love of the Trinity in her soul, lifting her up into the very life of God. Here was the source of all her power to give the Father a love worthy of Him. Meditating on this, she says: 'Oh, my Saviour, it is You whom I love, it is You who draws me so irresistibly to You, You who, descending into this land of exile, was willing to suffer and to die in order to lift up each single soul and plunge it into the very heart of the Trinity, love's eternal home'.

This precious truth was focussed to a point for her in the Blessed Sacrament, where the heavenly Father's love is made tangible and concrete for every one of His children.

Because of this the Blessed Sacrament was to her the very centre of her life. In it she found revealed all the secrets of that Father's love. 'Oh, my Saviour, You ascended into light inaccessible, yet You remain in the vale of tears under the appearance of a small white host in order to nourish our souls with Your own substance. Let me tell You that Your love runs even unto folly. Before such folly, how could You but desire that my soul should leap up to You'.

This, then, is the first foundation of the Little Way of Spiritual Childhood. To those who walk this Little Way all is love between the heavenly Father and His child; and it is precisely the little, childlike soul that, putting aside all other truths that might complicate its vision, goes straight to the heart of things and sees just the overwhelming truth of the Father's love. To the little soul the whole burden of Scripture is the coming down of the Father's love to dwell in the soul of His little child, and so lift it up to Him; and the whole of the Catholic Church, its Hierarchy and its Sacraments, exist for one purpose and one end, namely, the planting of that seed of divine love in each individual soul. And therefore it is the Blessed Sacrament which is, above all, the centre and the inspiration of the Little Way, because in it this truth is focussed to a point with such complete simplicity. And it is the little soul which, with its complete simplicity of outlook, sees this most directly; just as, in the case of a little child, the only thing it sees in its parent is love.

Humility

What is the next fact that stands out most clearly in the life of a little child? It is its dependence upon its mother, a dependence absolute and complete. If it lets go its mother's hand for a moment there is a disaster and the little one falls. Without the mother it can do absolutely nothing. Its sense of dependence is precisely in proportion to its littleness. Its only safety is to keep a firm hold of its mother's hand. If only it does this, its mother can lead it through perils, by which, if left to itself, it would be overwhelmed, and to heights which, by itself, it could never climb.

In the supernatural sphere this is theologically accurate. We are completely dependent upon our heavenly Father for everything, dependent upon Him for our physical existence and, what is far more, completely dependent upon Him for that life of union with Him for which He had made us. The dwelling of the Holy Trinity in our souls is His free gift. By ourselves we can do nothing. If we let go of divine grace we fall and there is disaster. 'Without me you can do nothing' (*Jn* 15:5). But if we keep our hand firmly in our heavenly Father's hand – that is to say, if we rely entirely on grace and surrender our wills completely to it – then the heavenly Father will lead us through perils which otherwise might overwhelm us and to heights of sanctity which, by ourselves, we could never climb. It is those who tread the Little Way of

Spiritual Childhood who see this most clearly, just because they are little souls. In the natural life it is the littleness of the little child that gives it its sense of dependence upon its mother, and it is the littleness of the little soul which enables it to realise its dependence upon the heavenly Father.

And what is littleness in a soul? It is humility. Humility is the virtue which enables us to see how utterly dependent we are upon the heavenly Father. And so St Thérèse loved humility above all else. It was the essential foundation of her Little Way. That is why the Little Way is so sure, so safe. Pride and humility in deadly conflict, that is the whole process of redemption. To be emptied of self so as to be filled with the divine love needs a new birth, a conversion. 'Unless you be converted and become as little children you cannot enter the kingdom of Heaven.' As pride is the root of all sin, making us think we can live independently of God and so separating us from Him, teaching us, in fact, to let go of the heavenly Father's hand, so humility is the foundation of all holiness, teaching us our essential dependence upon God, placing our hand once again firmly in that of the heavenly Father.

To realise her nothingness apart from God was St Thérèse's greatest joy. 'The Almighty has done great things for me, and the greatest is to show me my littleness and my helplessness for any good'. Nothing taught her her dependence so much as the knowledge of her own failings. 'I do not grieve in seeing that I am weakness itself. On the contrary, it is in this I glory; and I expect each day to discover new imperfections; and I acknowledge that these lights concerning my nothingness do me more good than the lights concerning the Faith.' And so St Thérèse learnt to be glad at the knowledge of her failings just because that taught her her littleness, which was so precious in her eyes because it was so precious to our Lord. 'That which pleases Jesus in my little soul is to see me love my littleness' – the littleness which enabled her to keep firm hold of her Father's hand.

This humility is no weak or negative thing. It is the most powerful thing in the world, for it is the key which unlocks the soul to grace. By ourselves we can do nothing to increase in us the supernatural love for which we were made, but by grace we help by removing that which is in the way of the divine love, namely, self-love. With every act of humility, every time we accept a humiliation lovingly, more of self is removed, and therefore there is more room for the divine love to dwell in the soul. The depth of the ocean depends upon the depth of the caverns that lie below, and the depth of supernatural love in a soul is exactly in proportion to the caverns that humility has wrought in the secret recesses of that soul. And so the Sacrament of Penance takes its place quite simply in the Little Way as the heavenly Father's plan for emptying the soul of self-love, enabling the little one to take firm hold of His hand again. The soul that is really humble and empty of self-love, surrendered to the love of God, is the soul of which Jesus can take full possession and carry through difficulties and up to heights which otherwise the soul would find impossible. That is why humility is the most powerful thing in the world.

That is what St Thérèse meant when she said: 'It is my weakness that makes all my strength. Jesus did everything in me. I did nothing but remain little and weak'. Thus the very thing that to many people seems to be weak and trifling, namely, the 'littleness' of the Little Way, is in reality its true strength, its very foundation. For the soul that is most humble is most filled with divine love, and that is the only true strength, the only real greatness. Our Lady was 'full of grace' because she was so perfectly humble, so empty of self. And because St Thérèse was so humble, so weak, therefore she is now so great a Saint in Heaven. Our heavenly Father points to her today, saying to us: 'Whosoever, therefore, shall humble himself as this little child, he is the greater in the Kingdom of Heaven'.

Confidence

From humility springs the next foundation of the Little Way of Spiritual Childhood. In the natural sphere, what is it that springs from the dependence of the little child? Out of its utter dependence springs an unquestioning confidence. Its very littleness gives it an intuitive sense of

confidence. It never occurs to the little child that its
mother could fail it. The result is that it plays in perfect
confidence at its mother's feet. On the mother's side the
utter dependence of the little child cries to her heart as
nothing else could do. One glance, one cry, and, if she is
a perfect mother, even before that cry is heard she is there
with her arms around her little one. That is the picture.
And the smaller the little child, the more watchful is the
mother to anticipate its every need.

It is exactly the same with the souls who tread the
Little Way of Spiritual Childhood. Out of their complete
dependence upon the heavenly Father there springs a
complete confidence in His love. The humble soul knows
that it has been made solely to love this heavenly Father,
that by itself it is powerless to do so, and that therefore
the heavenly Father has given the Holy Trinity to dwell in
the soul; and that He has given the Blessed Sacrament to
feed the soul, just in order that the soul may grow in its
love for Him. How then can that heavenly Father fail His
child, provided that that little child keeps humble and
little? 'Does a woman forget her baby at the breast, or fail
to cherish the son of her womb? Yet even if these forget,
I will never forget you' (*Is* 49:15). All the heavenly
Father needs is a look, a cry, a prayer, and He is there
with His arms round us. He will do all in us and for us if
only we remain little and humble.

Our Blessed Lord has committed Himself. He who said, 'Unless you be converted and become as little children, you shall not enter the kingdom of Heaven' is bound to come to the aid of all those who, for His sake, are trying to become humble and dependent souls.

The mysteries of our Holy Faith, which are the proofs to the little, humble soul of the heavenly Father's love, are also to the humble soul the grounds of its confidence. Bethlehem, Calvary, the Resurrection, the indwelling of the Holy Trinity in the soul, the Blessed Sacrament, all spell one word, Confidence. 'Since God did not spare his own Son, but gave him up to benefit us all, we may be certain, after such a gift, that he will not refuse anything he can give' (*Rm* 8:32). It was this that gave St Thérèse her invincible confidence. 'My Way is all love and confidence in God. I cannot understand those souls who are afraid of so tender a friend', 'What offends Jesus, what wounds Him to the heart, is our want of confidence.' 'We cannot have too much confidence in the good God, so mighty, so merciful'. What is it that destroys confidence in so many souls? It is an unchildlike fear of the heavenly Father's justice. With St Thérèse it was never so. In the Little Way there is indeed the true filial fear, but never the fear of God's justice which would rob the little soul of its confidence.

To St Thérèse the heavenly Father's love is supremely a merciful love. Just because she was so conscious of her littleness and weakness that she saw, with a clearness impossible to a soul less conscious of its weakness, that the supreme quality of the heavenly Father's love was its mercy. Her soul's delight was to meditate on the merciful love of God Incarnate stooping down to earth and reaching out to that which is weakest, most soiled, most miserable. That, to her, was the supreme motive of the merciful love of God, namely, pity for that which is weak. She knew her weakness would cry to the heavenly Father's mercy as nothing else could do. From this sprang her invincible confidence. She says: 'Indeed, I hope as much from the justice of God as from His mercy. It is because He is just that He is compassionate and merciful, long-suffering, plenteous in mercy. "For he knows our frame, he remembers that we are but dust." 'As the Father has compassion for his children, so has the Lord compassion for us'. 'What joy to think that our Lord is just, that He takes into account all our weaknesses and He knows perfectly all the frailty of our nature. How, then, can I be afraid?'

It is this clear vision of the merciful love of God which makes the Little Way so all-embracing. On the one hand it gives help and confidence to the greatest sinners just because they are such great sinners. 'It is not merely because I have been preserved from mortal sin that I lift up my heart to God in confidence and love. I am certain that, even if I had on my conscience every imaginable sin, I should lose nothing of my confidence, but would throw myself, heart-broken with sorrow, into the arms of my Saviour. I remember His love for the Prodigal Son; I have heard His words to Mary Magdalene, to the woman taken in adultery, and to the woman of Samaria. No, there is no one who could frighten me, for I know too well what to believe concerning His mercy and His love.'

But if, on the one hand, the Little Way gives confidence to great sinners, it also gives confidence to those who are tortured by scruples because of their little failings. In the natural sphere little children do not fall very far, and, if they do fall, they do not hurt themselves very much, and the mother's arms are round them almost before they fall. St Thérèse tells us it is the same in the spiritual sphere. The soul that is humble cannot fall very gravely. The heavenly Father is there, watching over it, ready to put His arms round it after every fall. 'I have long believed that the Lord is more tender than a mother. I have sounded the depth of more than one mother's heart and I know that a mother is ever willing to forgive the involuntary little failings of her child.' In fact, these little failings and miseries can be turned into a blessing, for they teach the little soul its weakness and so throw it back once more into its Father's arms. 'What does it matter to me to fall each moment? By that I feel my weakness and therein I find great profit. My God, you see what I can do if You do not carry me in your arms.'

Thus the Little Way is a way of complete trust and self-surrender to the merciful love of the Father. For the little soul knows that, whether its sins have been great or not, the heavenly Father who has created it solely to love Him cannot fail to give it all that it needs so long as it remains humble and penitent. This takes away all the Jansenist servile fear of God and, instead of walking in that fear, the little soul walks hand in hand with its heavenly Father with the radiant confidence of a little child. So walking, it is delivered from another fear also – the fear of the future. For one of the most precious fruits of this confidence is shown in the power to cease to worry about the future. It is right indeed to take every prudent precaution, but our Lord definitely says: 'Do not worry about tomorrow'. Anxiety about the future is one of the most fruitful sources of destruction of confidence in a soul. How many people are worn to shreds by fears of a future trouble which never comes, or of one which, if it does come, seldom comes in the way we fear it will.

The little child does not think beyond the day. It receives all it needs from its parents from moment to moment. This is exactly true of the life of the little soul. It lives from day to day. Every Christian knows the philosophy of living just for today; how, if we live for today, it lessens the power of our temptations, because we are tempted only for today; how it takes away the power of pain if we have to suffer only for today.

But St Thérèse, with her Little Way, throws completely new light on it. For she says that all this is secondary, that the real thing is to think of today as the only day we have in which to love God. What quality then will we put into our love!

My life is an instant, an hour which passes by,
My life is a moment which flies and is away,
You know, O my God, that to love You on this earth,
I only have today.

If we love Him today as though we had no other day in which to love Him, then of course, automatically, all our pain becomes easier to bear, all our temptations lose their strength. But it is the love which is the key to it all.

'I notice', she says, 'that our Lord does not give me provisions, but nourishes me from moment to moment with food that is ever new. I do not know how it happens, but I just believe that it is Jesus, hidden in the depth of my soul, inspiring me and giving me the power, moment by moment, to do what He wishes.' Once again we see the theology of the Little Way. For here is the doctrine of grace. We are not given grace for a tomorrow which may never come, but we are given grace which is never lacking, however feeble may be our response.

In her suffering at the end of her life she reveals that it was this which gave her so much strength. 'If I did not simply live from one moment to another it would be impossible for me to be patient, but I look only at the present. I forget the past and I take good care not to forestall the future. When we yield to discouragement or despair, it is usually because we think too much about the past or the future.' So she trod her Little Way with childlike confidence right to the end.

Love towards The Father

We have seen that the Little Way of Spiritual Childhood is all based on the heavenly Father's love. The little soul, created purely for the Father's love, moves among the path of spiritual childhood in complete dependence upon His goodness and His power. Now what response can the little soul make to that love? How can it co-operate with the heavenly Father's plan of love? In the natural sphere, what is the activity of the little child? Watch any little one with it's mother. How does it shows its love? By little things – just anything that comes across its path in its little world, a flower, a picture, or a toy – it takes it straight to its mother for her to see; something so small that it has no value except insofar as it expresses the love of the little one, which is so precious in its mother's eyes.

A little child relates everything to its mother in little acts of love. And, all the time, it can only do it because it's mother is there, watching it, supporting it with her care and ready to receive its offering. Without her its love would have no object; all would be chaos and confusion. In the Little Way of Spiritual Childhood it is precisely the same. The little soul can only co-operate with the Father's love, can only express its own love, by little things, by relating everything to the heavenly Father as an expression of its love. In other words, by doing everything to please the heavenly Father. St Thérèse tells us so herself. 'I have always been very little and I have never been able to do anything but very little things. How shall I show my love since love is proved by works? Well, the little child will strew flowers... No other means have I of proving my love than to strew flowers – that is, to let no little sacrifice escape me, not a look, not a word, to make use of the very least actions and do them all for love.'

She took every little incident, every joy, every disappointment and misunderstanding, everything that came her way, some little word or action, something easy, something difficult, she grasped each, as a little child plucks a flower, and laid it at our Lord's feet as an expression of her love for Him. 'I work for His pleasure alone'.

Here then is the way by which the little soul shows its love to the heavenly Father. It is so simple, so all-embracing. The greater part of our daily life is made up of little things, very ordinary things indeed; and the beauty of the Little Way is that it gathers in all these apparently unimportant things and fills them with a supernatural glory. The little soul, realising that it has been created by the heavenly Father solely to love Him and to be loved by Him, knows that all the circumstances of life in which it finds itself placed are therefore the setting ordained by the heavenly Father whereby the little soul is to express its love. This entirely puts an end to the temptation to divide our life into spiritual and secular, the temptation to think of God only when we are upon our knees and to forget Him in our work. Everything is an instrument to express our love; every humiliation taken patiently, every difficulty faced calmly, every sorrow borne courageously, every disappointment met bravely, every weary detail taken cheerily, every little duty in the home or business done to the best of our ability, all of these are offerings, little flowers by which to express our love to our heavenly Father.

Writing to her sister, the Saint says: 'It is the little things done for love which charm the heart of the good God'. So, here and now on earth, in little, unimportant things, begins that very life of Union, through supernatural love, which is to be our glory in heaven. This is precisely what theology teaches us, namely, that all creatures around us, all we meet in life, are to be used as means to glorify God through love; that all our life is just a means to our last end, love; and, apart from that last end, it has no meaning. And, just as the little child can only offer its little tokens of love to its mother because she is there, enveloping the little one with her love and protection, so the soul, though free, can only offer its acts of love through the power of God's grace.

St Thérèse was never tired of saying: 'I have never been able to do anything by myself'. The little soul makes these acts of love just as much in the grey days as in the days when all is bright and sunny. 'In times of dryness, when I am incapable of praying and practising virtue, I seek little opportunities, mere trifles, to give pleasure to Jesus; for instance, a smile, a pleasant word when inclined to show weariness. If I have no opportunities I at least tell Him again and again that I love Him. That is not difficult, and it keeps alight the fire of love in my heart.' Is there anybody who cannot do this, with a good will and with the help of grace? The Little Way once more is so safe, for it does not ask the little soul to do any great work. For the heavenly Father does not look at the greatness of the work, but at the love which lies behind it. 'Our Lord does not look so much at the greatness of our actions, nor even at their difficulty, as at the love with which we do them. What then have we to fear?'

Again, the little soul treads this Way with perfect confidence in its effort to show its love through little things. It knows it will often fail and make mistakes. But, in the natural life, if a little one brings a picture to its mother upside down, the mother does not punish the little one. She does not even trouble to turn the picture the right way up. She is not looking at the picture but at the

love of the little one behind it. And the little soul knows
that it is the same with the heavenly Father's love, and so
all temptations to scruples disappear.

Love towards one's neighbour

The Little Way is the source of all our love to those around
us. Next to our love for our heavenly Father comes our
love for our neighbour – those men and women with whom
we live our daily life. Just because the little soul realises, in
its utter simplicity, that the supreme relationship between
itself and the heavenly Father is love so, when it looks out
on those around, it sees them just as so many other little
children of the heavenly Father, created to love Him and to
be loved by Him. As the little soul loves the heavenly
Father, so it loves all His other children for His sake. That
is the only thing which concerns it. This at once lifts up
every relationship into the supernatural.

The source of St Thérèse's love to those around her
was the supernatural love which the heavenly Father
placed in the soul of His child. 'Oh, my Jesus, You never
ask what is impossible. You know I can never love my
sisters as You have loved them unless within me You love
them, dear Lord… Yes, I know when I show charity to
others it is simply Jesus acting in me, and the more closely
I am united to Him the more dearly I love my sisters.' So
only can the little soul fulfil our Blessed Lord's
commandment: 'Little children, love one another, as I

have loved you' (*Jn* 13:34). By this the little soul is saved from all those unworthy motives which destroy the peace of so many – jealousies, envies, criticisms, scandals.

In the natural life the little child is not concerned with the actions and motives of others except insofar as they affect its relationship to the heavenly Father. Apart from this, it is unmoved by their actions, their motives, their temperaments, whether they be attractive or otherwise. The little child does not judge. 'Is there anything more sweet', says St Thérèse, 'than the inward joy of thinking well of our neighbour?' This sounds too high an ideal for human nature. It is indeed only those souls who are little enough to see only the Father's love that can attain to it. The test of all this comes when the question concerns someone whom, naturally, we dislike, who gets on our nerves.

It is precisely here that the Little Way of St Thérèse was tested to the uttermost. She tells us so in her own words: 'A holy nun of our Community annoyed me in all she did. I did not want to yield to my natural antipathy, for I remembered that charity ought to portray itself in deeds and not to exist merely in feelings. So I set myself to do for this sister all I should do for the one I loved most... One day she said to me, with a beaming face: "My dear Sister Thérèse, tell me what attraction you find in me. Whenever we meet you greet me with such a sweet smile." Ah, what attracted me was Jesus hidden in the depths of her soul.' But it takes a very little soul, whose life is all based on love, humility, and confidence in the heavenly Father's love, to rise to such heights of charity as this. And yet it is exactly here, in these little daily things, that all is lost or won. What is all this but the simple Gospel teaching: 'Love your enemies and pray for those who persecute you; in this way you will be sons of your Father in heaven. Be perfect just as your heavenly Father is perfect' (*Mt* 5:44-48).

Love through Suffering

But what about suffering and sorrow and all the pain and evil of life? Has the Little Way any answer to this, the central tragedy of human existence? If not, it may be all right for angels, but it is no use for us men and women who have to live in a world where suffering is everywhere, within us and around us. How can we use our pain as a means of loving our heavenly Father? In the natural sphere, what is it that takes a little one to its mother quicker than anything else? Pain. Let a child hurt itself even but a little and it goes with its pain straight to its mother's arms. And in its mother's arms its pain is not taken away, but it finds something that makes the pain easier to bear – a sympathy, an understanding between the mother and the little child which no scientist can analyse nor can any philosopher define, but which is one of the most fundamental facts of human life.

This is exactly true of the Little Way. The little soul, offering every little thing in its daily life as an expression of

its love to its heavenly Father, soon comes across pain.
What does it do? Knowing that all is love between itself
and its heavenly Father, realising its utter dependence on
that love, certain in its confidence that the love can never
fail, seeing too that all its life is ordained to be a setting
whereby it may express its love, it at once seeks to find its
Father's love somewhere in its pain. In other words, it takes
its pain straight to its heavenly Father's arms. And, in that
Father's embrace, its pain is not taken away, but it finds
itself gathered into the mystery of a crucified God. That is
what St Thérèse did in her Little Way. In her earliest days
she came across pain and suffering. Instead of trying to bear
it by herself, and so letting it separate her from her heavenly
Father's love, she learnt to go with her pain straight to Him.
And there she found, what all the little souls who follow her
will also find, that the answer to pain lies in the arms of the
crucified God and nowhere else.

First she saw that suffering, so far from being wholly
bad, is a treasure, because our Blessed Lord chose it.
'Suffering is indeed a treasure because Jesus came down to
earth on purpose to possess it.' The pain of the little soul
interprets the pain of the Crucified and, from that, arises an
intimate friendship. All friendship has some ground in
common, and the common ground of this friendship is pain.
'For Him I have accepted the loss of everything... all I
want is to know Christ... and to share his sufferings' (*Ph*
3:8-10). That is the first stage. Then gradually this

fellowship merges into identity of life. St Thérèse puts this
very beautifully. 'Why does Jesus allow us to suffer?' she
asks. And then she gives the answer: 'Because He knows it
is the only means of preparing us to know Him as He
knows Himself, to become ourselves divine'. For the little
soul the supreme means of Union with Jesus is suffering.

Writing to her sister, St Thérèse says: 'Let us be one
with God even in this life, and to be so we should
embrace the Cross with joy'. Here is the second secret
which the soul learns in the embrace of its crucified
Lord – being taken up into the arms of our Saviour
upon His Cross, the little soul realises that it is not
following Him afar off, but that, as it unites its pain and
suffering with His, its life becomes merged with His
life. We find ourselves united with Him as we have
never before been united and, in a way we can never
explain, we see that, being with Him in it all, the whole
thing is changed; and we find it is He living in us, He
suffering in us. 'I have been crucified with Christ, and I
live now not with my own life but with the life of
Christ who lives in me' (*Ga* 2:19-20) – the Holy Trinity
living and loving in us in the midst of the pain and
darkness of Calvary in our souls.

Thus, just as with our Blessed Lord, pain, suffering, and
death were but the prelude to the resurrection: so with us,
pain, suffering, and death are but the avenue to that life of
union with our heavenly Father through supernatural love

from which our souls were made; and that, here and now. Only by dying to self can we live to Him.

Nor is this all. The little soul is drawn into a deeper mystery still. As it suffers with him, it shares not only in the pain of His Cross, but in the redemptive power of that Cross; and its sufferings, in union with His, call down from Calvary graces upon other souls. Writing to her sister, St Thérèse says: 'Let us offer our sufferings to Jesus for the salvation of souls'. In these simple words lies all the theology of St Paul regarding the mutual sufferings of the Mystical Body, whereby the sufferings of one member avail for the succour of another member in virtue of their union with their common head. 'It makes me happy to suffer for you, as I am suffering now, and in my own body to do what I can to make up all that has still to be undergone by Christ for the sake of his body, the Church (*Col* 1:24). It was this secret – that her pain and suffering were the supreme means of union between her soul and Our Blessed Lord, and were also the means of sharing in the redemptive work of His Cross – that made suffering and pain to her a most precious thing. 'Far from complaining to Jesus of the cross that He sends us, I cannot fathom the infinite love that has led Him to treat us thus'. Because of this her soul was filled with gratitude: 'I thank You, O my God, for all the grace You have bestowed on me, and particularly for having made me pass through the crucible of suffering'.

So she passed along her Little Way smiling always and with a song of joy on her lips. 'I will sing, I will always sing, even though I have to pluck my roses from amidst the thorns; and the sharper and the longer the thorns, the sweeter shall be my song'; no mere words, for, just because she was so little, so dependent on the heavenly Father's love, and therefore so completely confident in Him, that heavenly Father was able to draw her to Him through suffering which would have been impossible for her merely human flesh to bear. For eighteen months she was the victim of tuberculosis in its most painful possible form. The doctor who attended her said: 'If you only knew what she has to endure! I have never seen anyone suffer so intensely with such a look of supernatural joy'.

But, more even than this, her heavenly Father gave to her the further gift of spiritual desolation, which is so often the mark of His tender love for the saints. In talking to her sister St Thérèse describes this trial: 'If you were to judge by the poems I have composed this year, it must seem as though I had been flooded with consolations, like a child for whom the veil of Faith has almost been rent asunder: and yet it is not a veil, it is a wall which rises to the very heavens and shuts out the starry sky. When I sing of the happiness of heaven and the eternal possession of God, I do not feel any joy therein, for I sing only of what I wish to believe'. This suffering, physical and spiritual, lasted till the very end; but always she remained the heavenly Father's little child, resting in His arms, dependent and confident. In the moment of crisis, when the hour of her death drew near, the spirit of the Apostle shines through it all in her magnificent words: 'I could not have believed it was possible to suffer so intensely. I can only explain it by my intense longing to save souls'. A few hours later, she lifted herself a little on the pillow and, raising her eyes with a look of indescribable happiness and joy, she died.

Thus little Thérèse, that childlike soul which was chosen by God to show the Little Way of Spiritual Childhood to countless souls, has traced her Little Way for us, entering right into the heart of the world's most devastating problem, the problem of pain, and has shown us that it is only those souls who are little enough to go straight to their heavenly Father with their sufferings who can find their peace and joy in that which fills all others with despair. For 'Unless you be converted and become little children, you cannot enter into the kingdom of heaven'.

THE CROWN OF THE LITTLE WAY

Abandonment

When a little child, having taken its pain to its mother, finds safety and understanding in her arms, it rests there, calm and confident, completely surrendered to its mother's care. This picture of the little child, serenely cradled in its mother's arms, is a perfect parable of that abandonment to God which is the special fruit of the Little Way of love, humility, and confidence. When the little soul finds that even pain and suffering are all within the heavenly Father's love, are all precious gifts from the heavenly Father to His child, by which that child is cradled in His arms more securely than by anything else, it knows then that nothing can hurt it. Therefore it abandons itself completely to its heavenly Father's Will, confident that all is well so long as it rests, completely surrendered, in its Father's arms. 'Jesus was pleased to show me', says St Thérèse, 'the only path which leads to the divine love. This path is the abandonment of the little child who sleeps without fear in its Father's arms'.

Some people have misunderstood this imagery and think that the little soul thus depicted rests inert and lifeless in the arms of God. But what the little child does by instinct in the natural sphere, the soul must do by grace in the supernatural. The sleep of the little child is the parable of that peace which comes from a completely surrendered will, a will entirely surrendered from moment to moment. This demands continual activity, an activity comparable with the activity of a drowning man who, suppressing his natural instinct to trust in his own efforts, and realising that his only hope lies in abandoning himself, entirely and without resistance, to the man who swims to his rescue, completely surrenders himself – an act demanding the highest courage and the most perfect self-control.

That this abandonment is an active thing is apparent every time St Thérèse speaks of it. On the day of her Profession she prays: 'I offer myself to You, O my Beloved, that you may perfectly accomplish in me Your holy will'. A few years later, writing to her sister, she says: 'My desire is to do always the will of Jesus. Let us leave Him free to take and to give whatever He wills. Perfection consists in doing His will, surrendering ourselves wholly to Him'. 'The more content a soul is to accomplish His will, the more perfect it is.' This, so far from being easy, is one of the most difficult things to which a soul is called in the spiritual life. It demands a constant fidelity to grace, 'From my childhood these words of Job's delighted me: "Though he kill me, yet will I trust in him". But I confess it was long before I was established in this degree of abandonment. Now I am there. The Lord took me and placed me there.'

From this ceaseless activity issued her peace. 'To suffer peacefully is not always to find consolation in the suffering, for peace is not always accompanied by joy, not at least by sensible joy. To suffer with peace it suffices that we truly will all that God wills.' More than this, abandonment was, to her, her happiness and her joy. 'The only happiness here below is to make it our study ever to find delight in the path that Jesus appoints for us.' It was her joy because it left Our Lord completely free to act in her and through her. 'With what delight have I delivered up my will to Him. Yes, I want Him to make Himself master of all my faculties in such a way that my actions shall no longer be human or personal, but wholly divine, inspired, and directed by the spirit of love'. 'Should the little child fear the dark of the night, or complain at not seeing Him who carries her? Let her shut her eyes; it is the one sacrifice God asks. By remaining thus, the dark will cease to terrify her, and before long peace, if not joy, will re-enter her soul'.

From this we see, and it is most important that this should be understood, that the abandonment of the little soul is in no sense a gesture of despair, as the English word might lead us to suppose. It is, on the contrary, that act of reckless joy with which a little child flings itself into its mother's arms. Such is the philosophy of the little Saint whom God has chosen to guide us by her Little Way. This abandonment of hers was tested to the uttermost in the terrible spiritual desolation which her heavenly Father allowed her to pass through during her last illness. How does she meet it? With the absolute simplicity of a little child. Why, in the natural sphere, does a mother hide herself from her little one? Only in order that the little one may seek her all the more. And the moment the distress becomes too grievous for the child the mother reappears and all is well. We grown-ups call it hide-and-seek. To the Saint on her deathbed, in her childlike trust, the hiding of God's face could mean only this. She expresses it in her own inimitable way: 'He will get tired of making me wait sooner than I shall get tired of waiting.'

To keep surrendered to the will of God is thus a constant activity, a constant co-operation with the fidelity to grace. And when this co-operation is given in the spirit of complete abandonment, then there is activity within perfect rest, a continual surrender, resting in the arms of God. This is the secret of the quiet activity of the Catholic Church on earth, and the nearest approach to the life of the saints in heaven.

The Victim of Love

Such is the phrase which St Thérèse used to express the final consummation of the soul who treads in the Little Way. To her the Little Way was a martyrdom of love and the little soul a victim of love. At her Profession she prayed: 'O Jesus, I ask that for Your sake I may die a martyr. Give me martyrdom of soul or body, or rather give me both the one and the other'. During her last illness we find the same desire. What do these words 'victim' and 'martyrdom' mean on the lips of St Thérèse? To understand what this word 'victim' means, we must understand what St Thérèse understood as she knelt before the one perfect victim on the Cross. She saw Him, it is true, as a victim to the sins of men, paying the price man could not pay. That is true. But that is not the main thing that St Thérèse saw. Looking upon the Cross with the eyes of a little child, she saw something infinitely deeper, more primary, more profound. She saw on the Cross God Himself the victim of His own love. Why was He there? Because He is love and He cannot help loving. Even when that love is flouted and rejected by men, God goes on loving with that 'Divine Folly', as St Thérèse calls it, which drew Him to the manger and the Cross. And what exactly is the divine love doing? He has come down to the Cross to lift men up into the divine life and love, from which they had been separated by sin. And the marvel of the divine love is just this: that, in order to accomplish this, He uses the very results of men's sin, and separation from Him – namely, suffering, pain and death.

To St Thérèse the victim on the Cross was God the victim of His own merciful love. To her it was not so much 'God so desired to avenge sin that He sent His Son', as 'God loved the world so much that he gave His only Son, so that everyone who believes in Him may not be lost but may have eternal life' (*Jn* 3:16).

So, with the eyes of a child, she sees right through Jansenism to the fundamental thing – the love of Calvary, the love of the heavenly Father for His children. All the labour, the sweat and toil of the Cross is the labour of God's merciful love offering Himself as a victim, that by so doing He might once again fill men's souls with His own love, the love for which they were made, the love without which they are ever restless. In response to this love her ardent soul went out in generous longing to let this labour of love worked out on Calvary for all mankind be worked out to the full in her own individual soul, to offer herself as a little victim to be consumed by this divine love, so that, completely empty of all self-love, her soul might be flooded by the divine love.

She tells us in her autobiography how this desire took possession of her. 'In the year 1895 I received the grace to understand more than ever how much Jesus desires to be loved. Thinking one day of those who offer themselves as victims to the justice of God, in order to turn aside the punishment reserved for sinners by taking it upon themselves, I felt such an offering to be both noble and generous. I was very far nevertheless from feeling drawn to make it, and from the depths of my heart I cried: "O my divine Master, shall Your justice alone find atoning victims? Has not Your merciful love need of them also? On every side it is ignored and rejected, those hearts on which You would lavish it turn to creatures and seek their happiness in the miserable satisfaction of a moment, rather than cast themselves into Your arms, into the unfathomable furnace of Your infinite love. O my God! Must Your love which is disdained lie hidden in Your heart? It seems to me that if You should find souls offering themselves as a holocaust (as victims) to Your love, You would consume them rapidly and would be pleased to set free those flames of infinite tenderness now imprisoned in Your heart. If Your justice which avenges itself on earth must needs be satisfied, how much more must Your merciful love desire to inflame souls, since Your mercy reaches even to the heavens. O Jesus, permit that I may be that happy victim – consume Your holocaust (victim) with the fire of Your divine love".'

And now what exactly does she mean?

By this word 'victim' St Thérèse meant a complete offering of oneself to the divine love with the desire that all self-interest and self-seeking should disappear through the power of this all-absorbing love. She used this expression 'victim of love' in contrast to that of 'victim of justice'. It sprang from her lips in a spontaneous outburst of her heart, an outburst so tender that it longed that the most beautiful attribute of God – His love – should not be less thought of than His justice, which for so long had its victims.

She did not dedicate herself then to exceptional sufferings. She saw one thing only – love. 'The most excellent gift.' It is to the merciful, that is to say, sweet and compassionate, love of the good God to which she abandons herself, with the one desire of loving Him and making Him loved, without any thought of herself, or what should happen to her. She is just the child who surrenders itself to the Father's will to suffer or to rejoice just as His love shall decide. In this there is no room for sentimentalism. To dedicate oneself as a victim of love is not to be dedicated to sweetness and consolation: because love in this world lives only by sacrifice.

Thus suffering, in the Little Way, is always the avenue of love. In fact it is the re-entry to the fullness of love. This at once disposes of all morbidity or any desire for suffering as an end in itself. The condition of all supernatural life is the complete dying of self and birth into love which is the work of Calvary in the individual soul. 'Unless a wheat grain falls on the ground and dies, it remains only a single grain; but if it dies, it yields a rich harvest. Anyone who loves his life loses it; anyone who hates his life in this world will keep it for the eternal life' (*Jn* 12:24-25). It is the complete taking possession of the soul by the heavenly Father's love so that, emptied of self, it may be filled with that divine love, caught up into the divine love. The more completely the little soul is consumed by the divine love, the more it is transformed into the divine life of union with God through love.

Thus God crowns the abandonment of His little child: thus, abandonment makes all things sweet. And this is all worked out through just the little things of everyday life which the heavenly Father presents to us, His children, a little means of sacrifice whereby we may become completely victims of His love. In the Little Way of Spiritual Childhood the little soul does not ask for suffering, but gladly welcomes all that the Father gives. It is this complete abandonment of the little victim that shines out so wonderfully in the last illness of the Saint, and enabled her to bear indescribable pain with joy. Her sisters said to her: 'Your sufferings are terrible'. She replied: 'No, they are not terrible. Can a little victim of love find anything terrible that is sent her by her Spouse? Each moment He sends me what I am able to bear and nothing more, and, if He increases the pain, my strength is increased as well. But I could never ask for greater sufferings. I am too little a soul. They would then be of my own choice, I should have to bear them all without Him, and I have never been able to do anything when left to myself.'

A few days before her death she said to her sister: 'Do not be troubled if I suffer much and show no sign of peace at the end. Did not Our Lord Himself die a victim of love, and see how great was His agony!' Almost her last words were: 'Yes, all that I have written about my thirst for suffering is really true. I do not regret having surrendered myself to love'. Then, looking at her crucifix, she said: 'Oh, I love Him. My God... I love...You'. These were her last words. Suddenly she raised herself, as though called by a mysterious voice, and opening her eyes, which shone with an unutterable happiness and peace, she surrendered her soul into the heavenly Father's arms, to the end His little child.

EPILOGUE

'I entreat You to let Your divine eyes rest upon a vast number of little souls. I entreat You to choose in this world a legion of little victims of Your love.' Such is the prayer with which St Thérèse concludes her autobiography. These words were written by the little Saint hidden away in Carmel. Today, from Heaven, she looks to us to satisfy her longing. We have seen her face her Little Way of Spiritual Childhood, the Little Way that is possible for us all if only we will walk in the path of complete humility and utter confidence in our heavenly Father's love, using everything that He sends across our paths as a means of loving Him and those around us, surrendering ourselves to His merciful love with the complete abandonment of a little child.

This shows us clearly why the Holy Father teaches us that the Saint has been raised up with a special message of our time. Into the complexity of our age she comes with her simple vision of the Father's love. To the spirit of pride and independence she opposes the humility and dependence of a little child. To an age in which, just because of their independence, men and women have ceased to trust themselves and one another she brings that unquestioning confidence in God upon which all human trust depends. To an age which is impressed solely by the spectacular and the sensational she shows how real greatness is to be found in littleness and in being hidden. Finally, she shows us all that the only way to escape from the slavery of self is to become a victim of the divine love.

In all this there is nothing new. God has simply chosen this little Saint to take us back to what He Himself taught us when He was on this earth. 'Unless you change and become like little children, you will never enter the kingdom of heaven' (*Mt* 18:3).

O God, who inflamed with the spirit of love the soul of Your servant, Thérèse, grant that we also may love You and may make You greatly loved.

(Adapted from a prayer of the Saint)

St Thérèse's Act of Oblation

'That my life may be one act of perfect love, I offer myself as a victim of holocaust to Your merciful love, imploring You to consume me unceasingly, and to let the flood-tide of infinite tenderness, pent up in You, flow into my soul, so that I may become a very martyr of Your love, O my God.

'May this martyrdom, having first prepared me to appear before You, break life's thread at last, and may my soul take its flight unhindered to the eternal embrace of Your merciful Love.

'I desire, O my Beloved, at every heart-beat to renew this oblation an infinite number of times till the shadows fade away and I can tell You my love eternally face to face.'